The Very First CHRISTMAS

PAUL L. MAIER
ILLUSTRATED BY FRANCISCO ORDAZ

CONCORDIA PUBLISHING HOUSE · SAINT LOUIS

2   3   4   5   6   7   8   9   10   11   12   11   10   09   08   07   06   05   04   03

Children's Christmas books are often long on fancy but short on fact. Many of them ignore the central theme of the first Christmas and opt instead for Grimm's fairy-tale settings, quaint old European towns, or wondrous winter tableaus. The many yuletide stories about dour woodcarvers, sullen cobblers, or Ebenezer Scrooges who are transformed by the spirit of Christmas are certainly heartwarming, even if predictable, but too often the great Source of the "spirit of Christmas" is overlooked.

These pages, instead, will seek to return the Christmas focus to where it belongs. The setting is in America's mountainous west, where a mother—wife of a forest ranger—tells her bright eight-year-old son about the Nativity. Because of their secluded location, the boy has not attended Sunday school regularly, and his mother must answer the real questions he—and perhaps many like him—has about "the *very first* Christmas …"

Paul L. Maier

Chris wanted to know everything about everything. At school his teachers sometimes called him "Christopher Question Mark" because he was always raising his hand in class to ask for more information. And more information was never enough.

Chris still liked bedtime stories, to be sure, but he was always a little disappointed that fairy tales and such never *really* happened.

"From now on," Chris announced to his mom one night, "I want you to tell me stories about *real* people and *real* things that *really* happened."

"Well, all right," Mom replied, realizing that her eight-year-old was growing up. "But I thought you liked stories that ended with 'And they lived happily ever after.' "

"Sure! That's fine—as long as *the people* really lived."

"All right, then," Mom said with a little smile. "I see you want facts—not fantasy. I'll work on it."

The week before Christmas, Christopher's mother had an idea. She did a little reading on her own. Then she bought a simple nativity set and placed it by her son's bed. That evening at bedtime she said, "Now, Christopher, you said you wanted to hear *real* stories, not something made up?"

"Right, Mom!" he said emphatically.

"Well, Christmas is coming. Would you like to hear the true story of the first Christmas?"

"Oh, Mary and Joseph? And baby Jesus? I think I already know it."

"Maybe not everything, my boy. But let's try you out."
Mother rested her chin on her fingertips and thought for a
moment. Then she said, "All right, who is the first person
mentioned in the second chapter of Luke's gospel, the famous
story about the birth of Jesus?"

Chris reached for the figurine of a young girl. "The Virgin
Mary," he said with authority.

"Close, but she's in chapter one. It's Caesar Augustus.
Here—let's read it together." Christopher's mom opened their
family Bible to Luke 2.

In those days Caesar Augustus issued a decree that a census should be taken of the entire Roman world. (This was the first census that took place while Quirinius was governor of Syria.) And everyone went to his own town to register.

"Was our month of August named for this Augustus?" Chris wondered.

"Yes indeed, smart guy. Just as July was named for his great-uncle, Julius Caesar. Augustus was the first of the Roman emperors—some say the best. He brought peace and great prosperity to the whole empire. Even to far-off Palestine where Mary and Joseph lived.

"And, Chris, I think the reason Luke mentions Caesar Augustus first in the Christmas story is for exactly the same reason that you asked me to tell you true stories from now on and not fairy tales. God wants us to know that all this *really happened*, that it isn't just a story someone dreamed up. Everyone knows about the great Augustus and about the way he counted and taxed the people in his empire."

"What was that business about going back to the hometown to register?" Chris asked.

"Well, nowadays we have to register in our neighborhoods before we can vote, don't we? So Joseph had to go back to his hometown—Bethlehem—to register for the census. Here, you read on, Chris."

Chris picked up the Bible and read.

So Joseph also went up from the town of Nazareth in Galilee to Judea, to Bethlehem the town of David, because he belonged to the house and line of David.

Chris dropped the Bible. "Why didn't Mary go along?"

"She did, Christopher! Read first. Ask questions later!"

"Oh." Chris continued reading.

He went there to register with Mary, who was pledged to be married to him and was expecting a child.

"Now wait a minute," he frowned. "Don't people have to get married first and then have children?"

"That's the way it's supposed to be," Mom smiled, knowing that Chris would not fail to ask this question. "But Joseph was not the father of this baby. The father was not a man."

"What!" Christopher's jaw sagged open. "Who *was* the father then?"

His mom took a deep breath. "The father of this baby was—God Himself."

"*God* was the father? But why?"

"You see, Chris, when God first made people, He made them in His image—perfect, like Himself. But when Adam and Eve disobeyed God, sin came into the world. God's love is so great, He planned to save us by sending His own Son *to become one of us* and give His life for us. The greatest thing you'll ever learn, Chris, is that God became a human being in Jesus Christ—yes, in that little baby Mary was expecting."

Chris was quiet for a long moment, staring through his bedroom windows at the forest surrounding their home. A gentle dusting of snow fell on the trees. Finally, he managed to whisper, "God—in a *baby!* How do we know that?"

Mom smiled and held up the Bible. "From His Word. From the extraordinary things Jesus did when He grew up."

"But why did God choose Mary? How old was she? Where did she live?"

"One question at a time!" Mom laughed. "Okay, the last first. Mary came from a town called Nazareth up in Galilee—that was in the north country of Palestine. It was a beautiful area—mountains, hills, and fruitful valleys. And a huge lake too. The Sea of Galilee they called it."

"As big as Lake Tahoe, when we went to California?" Chris asked.

"Almost. And Mary's age? We don't know for sure, but in those days, girls got engaged and married at about 16 or 17. Their husbands were a little older. They had to build up a family nest egg before thinking of marriage."

"But why did God choose *Mary* to be Jesus' mother and not someone else?" Christopher persisted.

"We don't have all the answers, hon!" Mom laughed. "But why not Mary? In the first chapter of his gospel, Luke tells how the angel Gabriel announced the awesome news about Jesus to Mary. Luke calls her a girl who was 'highly favored' in God's sight. She agreed to become Jesus' mother in total faith and trust in God. What a marvelous young woman she was!"

Chris thought it over. "What about Joseph?"

"Joseph, God tells us, was a carpenter. A book I looked at said the Greek word for *carpenter* in the New Testament—*tekton*—can mean any craftsman working in the building business. So Joseph might have been not only a carpenter but a stonecutter too. Both he and Mary were descended from the royal line of King David in the Old Testament."

Chris sighed. "So they were royalty. A prince and princess—just like the fairy tales."

"No, hardly that! King David married quite a few wives and had children by them, so *many* people at the time of the first Christmas were actually related to King David. But here, I'll read on."

While they were there, the time came for the baby to be born, and she gave birth to her firstborn, a son.

"What time was that?" Chris interrupted. "The time when the baby was born. Morning? Night? December 25? The year 1?"

Mom laughed and explained, "We really don't know the exact time or date, but it was probably late afternoon or evening—you'll learn why when we read on. And December 25, I understand, was named the 'date for Christmas' more than 300 years *after* Jesus was born, so it might not be the exact date. But we do know that Jesus was born around 5 B.C. and not the year 1."

"Wait a minute. Jesus was born five years *before Christ?* That doesn't make sense."

"I knew you'd say that." Mom ruffled Chris' hair. "About 500 years after Jesus was born, a Christian monk re-did the calendar in the form we still use today. But he was mistaken by four or five years. So we know that about 2,000 years ago, probably some time between July and December, Jesus was born. But let me go on reading."

She wrapped Him in cloths and placed Him in a manger, because there was no room for them in the inn.

"Now a manger, Chris, is a feeding trough for animals ..."

"I know. Just like the one we have for our horses. So Jesus was born in a stable?"

"God's Word doesn't tell us it was a stable. But since Luke uses the word *manger*, we assume that it was. One of the earliest church fathers wrote that Jesus was born in a cave—a cave that was used as a stable. The area around Bethlehem today has many such places."

"Have they ever found the cave where Jesus was born?"

"Probably so. For at least the last 1,900 years, Christians have pointed to a cave or grotto beneath the Church of the Nativity in Bethlehem as the very place where Jesus was born."

"I'd love to see that," said Chris, his eyes sparkling as brightly as the stars outside. But then he pouted. "Still, a stable is a *miserable* place to have a baby—if you're not a cow or a horse, that is!"

"Why couldn't they have stayed with relatives or friends?" Chris continued. "Or at least in something like a motel?"

"Aha!" Mom laughed. "I think you answered your own question. Remember our vacation last summer, when Dad kept driving into the evening and we didn't call ahead for reservations? Remember how all the motels that night had 'No Vacancy' signs?"

"Yes," Chris remembered.

"It could have been something like that. We do know that when Wise Men arrived in Bethlehem later on, Mary, Joseph, and Jesus were living in a *house*, not a cave or stable. It's clear that they found a better place to stay after Jesus was born."

"Just like all the 'Vacancy' signs we saw the next morning on our trip!"

"Right you are," Mom laughed. Together they read the rest of Luke's great history of the first Christmas—how it all became public in a very short time.

And there were shepherds living out in the fields nearby, keeping watch over their flocks at night. An angel of the Lord appeared to them, and the glory of the Lord shone around them, and they were terrified. But the angel said to them, "Do not be afraid. I bring you good news of great joy that will be for all the people. Today in the town of David a Savior has been born to you; He is Christ the Lord. This will be a sign to you: You will find a baby wrapped in cloths and lying in a manger."

"Why were the shepherds terrified?" Chris wondered. "They should have been glad to be part of the Christmas story."

"Think, Chris," explained his mother. "You are going about your business at night when the sky suddenly opens up, light pierces the darkness, and a dazzling being you've never seen before starts talking to you!"

"I guess you're right. It's a wonder the shepherds didn't lose it."

"Especially after what followed." Mom went on reading.

Suddenly a great company of the heavenly host appeared with the angel, praising God and saying, "Glory to God in the highest, and on earth peace to men on whom His favor rests."

When the angels had left them and gone into heaven, the shepherds said to one another, "Let's go to Bethlehem and see this thing that has happened, which the Lord has told us about."

So they hurried off and found Mary and Joseph, and the baby, who was lying in the manger. When they had seen Him, they spread the word concerning what had been told them about this child, and all who heard it were amazed at what the shepherds said to them. But Mary treasured up all these things and pondered them in her heart. The shepherds returned, glorifying and praising God for all the things they had heard and seen, which were just as they had been told.

"And that, Christopher," said Mom, "is St. Luke's story of the very first Christmas. Did you like it?"

Chris had a faraway look in his eyes. But he slowly nodded his head.

"Remember," Mom added, "it's more than just a story or a tall tale. All of this really happened."

Christopher wrinkled his forehead in thought. "But how did Luke know all of this stuff? Was he there? He didn't say he was in the cave with Joseph and Mary, did he?"

"No."

"Then if he wasn't there, how could he ever write about it?"

"A very good question, my young scholar!" Mom exclaimed. "Let's see if you can find the answer. It's in the last part of the Christmas story."

Chris read the part about the shepherds again. Then he said, "The shepherds went away, spreading the word about Jesus. Maybe Luke heard it from them."

"Well, perhaps—many years later. But look again. Who else could have told Luke?"

Chris looked again at the Bible, and his eyes widened. "Yes. 'Mary treasured up all these things and pondered them in her heart.' So Mary probably told Luke all about what had happened!"

"Exactly. Some people think that Mary told Luke what had happened many years before. I told you she was an extraordinary woman. And God Himself told Luke the words He wanted written about His Son. Now it's time for sleep, Chris. Pleasant dreams."

Chris lay in his bed, thinking of all he had learned.
One thing he knew for sure. Real stories—especially God's
story—were certainly better than fairy tales.